Living After Losing

Dare to Live

Bernice Hill-Shepherd

Living After Losing

All scripture quotations marked (KJV) are from the Holy Bible, King James Version, in the public domain.

Scripture quotations marked (NIV) are taken from the Holy Bible, New International Version®, NIV®. Copyright © 1973, 1978, 1984, 2011 by Biblica, Inc.® Used by permission of Zondervan. All rights reserved worldwide. www.zondervan.com The "NIV" and "New International Version" are trademarks registered in the United States Patent and Trademark Office by Biblica, Inc.®

Scripture quotations marked (NKJV) taken from the New King James Version®. Copyright © 1982 by Thomas Nelson. Used by permission. All rights reserved.

Scripture quotations marked (NLT) are taken from the Holy Bible, New Living Translation, copyright ©1996, 2004, 2015 by Tyndale House Foundation. Used by permission of Tyndale House Publishers, a Division of Tyndale House Ministries, Carol Stream, Illinois 60188. All rights reserved.

Printed by:
Claire Aldin Publications
P. O. Box 453
Southfield, MI 48037
www.clairealdin.com

Library of Congress Control Number: 2020910082

ISBN 9781734746914 (paperback)

Printed in the United States.

In Memory Of...

This book is dedicated to my mom, Aslee Kelly, a woman
full of grace and compassion. Her beautiful and energetic
spirit will be missed by everyone who knew her.
Love you dearly, mom.

To the love of my life, Edward E. Shepherd.
Love and miss you!!

Living After Losing

Table of Contents

Living After Losing

Introduction

The biggest mistakes in life are not what we do, but what we fail to do. In the chapters ahead are milestones of inevitable moments which have allowed me to grow. At the same time, I realized how God designed all of us on purpose to be who we are.

Taking the right road doesn't always happen by faith, sometimes we take the path that feels right, rather the one that will eventually get us there. When we fail, and sometimes we do, we realize that failure is a good thing. God is trying to help us get it right. His undeserved generosity directs our steps through some of the most devastating events in our lives and no matter how hard we try to deter from the patterns of life, through His grace, we always get there. It's nothing more than being able to feel the joy of knowing that our hurt is much more than merely a feeling. I have realized that while going through the many challenges of life, while we are trying to figure it out - He has already worked it out.

Sometimes, we get into the habit of letting life happen to us. Instead of allowing what happens to be channeled into wisdom, strength, encouragement and understanding, we allow circumstances to push us into areas where we feel confined. When we began to realize that we can no longer do it alone, but need to trust God. He then stretches us to make us more versatile. He wants us to get into purpose!

Finally, our "Aha" moment allows us to look back and realize that He had us all the time. While traveling what seems like an endless road towards God's purpose for our lives, the road simply becomes both challenging and rewarding. I truly believe that when we share who we are today versus our yesterday; it is our testimonies that show how God can bless us despite our journey. It equally shows us how He brings redemption and renewal into our life. Let's build ourselves up, so when the storms of life come, our house will not fall.

The unfolding appetite of getting it right, after losing, is the new beginning of MY newly found journey as I witness God's grace, mercy, and love.

God is my source and in Him I move, I breathe...

~Bernice Hill-Shepherd

My Truth

Living After Losing

Twenty-one years later, I still remember that morning so very clear…

Returning home from the hospital after giving birth to our son, we were all so excited with our new family and were ready to begin our new journey. My daughter was left to sleep over at my sister's house; my husband and I were home alone with our newborn and my stepson (from a previous marriage). Due to complications, I had delivered our son via an emergency C-section. My husband had to assist me whenever I needed to get up from lying down due to the extreme amount of pain I was encountering.

On this particular morning, after my husband helped me out of bed, I noticed he was no longer in the bedroom. As time passed, I heard the bed in my daughter's room move. I vaguely remember calling out, "Edward what are you doing?" He responded, "I am not doing anything Hill, I am just relaxing." (He always called me by my maiden name, Hill.) Although, it seemed a bit strange that Edward mentioned he was relaxing at 2:00 a.m., when we usually relax together, I let it go. A few minutes later, I called out again, "Are you sure you're okay?" He answers, "I'm fine, Hill…go back to sleep", but, of course I did not. I struggled out of bed and went into my daughter's room. My husband was kneeling on the side of my daughter's bed holding his chest. At this point, everything started moving extremely fast.

Edward denied that he was in pain or that anything was wrong. I began probing, trying to encourage him back to bed, but something just didn't seem right. Finally, I exclaimed, "I'm calling the ambulance!" Something was surely wrong, but Edward insisted that everything was okay. He asked that I take him to the hospital instead of calling the ambulance. I called out for our son to pull the car out of the garage, while rushing out with Edward and grabbing a blanket for the baby. Edward wanted to make it down the stairs alone, but by the time he made it to the car, I was still at the top of the stairs with the baby moving very slowly. Suddenly, I watched my husband attempt to open the car door and began falling in what seemed like slow motion. I moved as fast as I could down the high steps of our condo. My step son was crying and screaming hysterically. I tried to remain calm as I placed the baby in the car seat and began to administer CPR, while calling out to my son **"GO CALL 911!"**

He was frantic, as he should be. Finally, I screamed out to him again, "Get in sync and please call 911!" He tried so hard to pull himself together and called 911. What seemed like an extremely long time, the ambulance finally arrived and took over the CPR procedure. Immediately, I began praying. My heart told me something was wrong - they seemed to have stayed there for so long...I tried to keep my focus and kept praying because, it could also mean something good. I asked again, if everything was okay; they assured me that he would be fine and placed my husband in the ambulance. I asked my step son to ride along with his dad, while I prepared the baby and bag for the drive to the hospital.

While preparing to drive, I telephoned my mom and sisters to let them know that we were on our way to the hospital and to please come. During the entire time while getting the baby ready, I continued to pray in the spirit asking God to protect my husband and keep us close to the cross. I reminded Satan, that I was ruling and reigning, he no longer had authority over me or anyone in my family. My God! I felt so overwhelmed; my heart felt as though something was not right. I began to replay the nightmare, to ensure that I had done everything within my power. As my mind raced, I thought "Oh my! I forgot to pray for the doctors and for the Holy Spirit to be in that emergency room with my husband. I continued to hold on and reminded myself, that all was well.

Once I arrived at the hospital, my step son came out to me screaming at the top of his lungs, "He's gone, my dad is gone!" I could do nothing but break down and cry out, "Don't you dare say that! Don't say that!" The nurses ran towards me and began asking a swarm of questions. "Is the baby a newborn? How are you both doing?" They brought a wheelchair for me to sit while they continued to ask questions in a manner that indicated, they wanted to ensure that the baby and I were okay. My step son was on his phone. Everything else, once again, seemed to be spinning out of control - I thought my heart was going to stop. All I wanted was for Edward to get up. No, I wanted to wake up.

This absolutely was not a dream and I could not believe I was here. I began praying again, asking God to give me strength. Heaven knows, I needed it. I was not prepared mentally or spiritually. I began quoting one of my favorite scriptures, "God is faithful, he will not let you be tempted beyond what you can bear" (I Corinthians 10:13). At this particular time, all I felt was my world crumbling right in front of me. The pain was indescribable...I wanted nothing more than for Edward to get up and walk out of the hospital with me. My knees felt weak and the excruciating pain from the C-section was killing me. My stepson was crying uncontrollably and there was nothing I could do. I wanted so badly to console him, but was having such a hard time keeping it together, and too busy trying to find myself. How could I?

My immediate family arrived quickly, but I still felt as though a big part of me was gone and absolutely nothing else mattered. I have no idea how long we waited. My family sat in the waiting room. My oldest sister and I awaited in the patient's area where Edward's body laid. I didn't want to leave him. I remember asking my sister, "What do we do now?" She looked into my eyes saying, "You do not have to do anything; stay here as long as you like." My sister is one of my best siblings ever. I have no idea what I would have done without her - thank you sis. I literally broke down in tears knowing that Edward would not be leaving the hospital - my husband would not be coming home. Wow! I didn't know what to do, how to feel, or how to comprehend it all.

Eventually, we all left the hospital. I attempted to pray, but nothing seemed to come out. I couldn't focus and everything was just spinning in my head. I cried out, *"Lord help me, but most importantly, equip me spiritually right now - in the things that will give me strength. Father, I thank you for it right now, whatever it may be, Lord because I know, you know what I need Father God."* Nothing else seemed to help me with this challenge. I tried so very hard to stay balanced, but continued to have a difficult time. It felt as if God could no longer hear me, yet I needed Him more than ever. Every thought was of Edward; no longer could I hold in the pain and finally, I went in to the "helpless zone".

I cried and cried.

"My flesh and my heart faileth, but God is the strength of my heart, and my portion forever" (Psalms 73:26 KJV)

Living After Losing

The Struggle

Living After Losing

When it comes to the waltz of human suffering - whether engaged in the dance or simply on the side-line observing, most of us are less than grateful. Sometimes, dear friends ignore their lifelong besties because they don't know how to respond after they suffer from loss which leads to devastating outcomes. Even sometimes, well-meaning people may clumsily attempt to encourage the grieving by musing out loud that "God must have needed another flower in His garden" or that "The Lord giveth and He taketh away." At the end of the day, it's not about someone else's perception. It's about us finding the balance and staying in the reality of who we are. God's plan for our lives are not always ours.

In Proverbs, Lord, Your word says wisdom flows in the street. This morning, Father, I ask you for your wisdom and understanding. Saturate me with your wisdom, so that I will know what and when to do what your will is Lord.

Despite my prayers, the feelings of uncertainty began to set in. I was afraid and uncertain of how my life was supposed to go on without my husband. Calling out to God became my number one; I knew in my heart that He was able. I began to shut everything out and as time passed, things were getting better.

A few weeks later, I started having headaches. The doctor prescribed medications for elevated blood pressure (BP) although I'd never had high BP. I knew that my body was feeling a little different, but never did I expect high BP. I tried coping by following the doctor's orders and trying to have peace by staying home and focusing on my little ones. The only other place that gave me a little more comfort was at my mom's home, but even staying there began to close in on me. I began to blame myself for listening to Edward and not calling the ambulance earlier, wishing that I had known that he was in trouble on *that* level. I was angry at the fact that he wasn't honest as to what he was feeling - he had to have known that he was having some serious pain. The doctor mentioned that he knew something wasn't right because of the excruciating pain, but there was no way that Edward could have known it was a massive heart attack.

Looking back, I remember Edward was never one to complain or show emotion when he wasn't feeling well or when something wasn't right. I always had to call it, by noticing his eyes were red when he would miss his meds. Maybe being released from the hospital in less than eight hours played a role in me missing it. Playing the scene back, I couldn't figure out how. My mind was racing...all I could do was ask God for strength. There was no one else who could help me now.

I began to wonder about the phrase "It gets better with time". Unfortunately, time had passed and it wasn't getting much better. Family and friends seemed to have moved on but as for me, I felt that I was the only person stuck. Edward's son and I together seemed to be having a difficult time trying to grasp it all and move forward. It was the hardest thing I ever had to do. I had no idea how I was supposed to move on, especially with a very interval part of my family gone. At times, I wasn't quite sure if I wanted to move on. I truly wanted to die. *Yes, I wanted to die!*

Although, I had the children, for some reason it just didn't seem to be enough. I wasn't ready to accept my loss and coping seemed more difficult than I expected. *I just wasn't ready!* My entire life had changed and there was nothing to be done. For several months I shut down and distanced myself from most of the world. In my heart, I still knew that despite it all, God was faithful, but in my heart, it was a different story. I couldn't drown out the noise from my ears; the devil was busy. I just didn't realize how busy he was at the time.

Never did I expect my life with my husband would end this soon - the dreams, plans, and goals we wanted to accomplish together with our children. Now, I wonder, how in the world was I going to make it all fall in place? For some reason, everything seemed to be falling apart, but I continued to remain faithful. Our timing is not that of God's, and we do not always understand why He does what he does, nor do we always understand the lessons. But, one thing I know for sure, He is faithful and although it doesn't feel or look like it at the time, our God provides. In knowing this, we have to completely submit and trust Him - not mediocre trust, but to fully trust Him. I struggled with this at first, but knowing that I had to trust God completely in an effort to get me through, was my constant focus. You know, it's easy to say, "I trust Him," but do we truly trust him completely? Eventually, we all have to remember that He, above all, is our strength and through him all things are possible.

"A father to the fatherless, a defender of widows, is God in his holy dwelling." (Psalm 68:5 NIV)

The Challenge of Keeping My Eyes on Him

Living After Losing

My grandmother always said, not to question God although, in many of the Bible stories God was questioned. So instead, I continued to maintain my composure by trying to stay balanced, which was usually easy for me, but today, for some reason I absolutely could not. I was unable to do anything... just wanted to stay in the bed. When the phone rang, I would not answer. When family and friends came by, I avoided them by not answering the door. I was absolutely in my feelings and did not want to do anything. Instead, I focused on taking care of the children and listening to my gospel music. Music has the power to uplift, as well as calm and ease; they say, "Music soothes the body and mind". I'm one to agree, as I praise God and ask for directions, I remind myself to stay focused. The word teaches us to *"lean not on our own understanding."* I clearly understood this passage, because I could not phantom what was happening and/or why at this time.

Have you ever felt like, "Not now Lord, please do not make me go through this!" Feelings of disconnect from everything around you and all you want is for it all to go away, but you realize at some point that you have to deal with it. I felt as though there was nothing left for me anymore. When we grieve, at some point, there may not be any logical thinking; all we want is for the pain to end. As for me, I did not consider the children or the rest of my family - coping at this time was out of the question. This episode was much harder than I expected.

My spiritual life at this time had fallen a little short; however, my prayer life was still on par. Although, the many challenges of trying to remain balanced was beginning to get harder as time passed, I realized that this journey had just begun. Trying to cope with a loss could be one of the hardest things in life. Timing absolutely can make things appear worst - while trying to stay balanced with the new addition to the family (my son), the upkeep of our home, financial balance, job, and my six year old daughter. Nevertheless, I'm still amazed at how God was able to turn my adverse situation around through His grace.

A few months later, I couldn't hear God anymore and Trinity Broadcasting Network (TBN) was no longer reaching me; I needed to get rid of the noise. Finally, I realized that I was getting in a rut and something had to give. My mind was racing with all sorts of thoughts. TBN was my go-to channel when I missed church for whatever reason. In an effort to rid all the noise, whispers and negative thoughts, I began to pray. *Father God, help me to hear your voice - give me the strength to get control of myself. Help me to see, Father, direct my steps, Lord; help me to find my balance through this dark and challenging place.* I constantly rebuked all the lies and negative energy I was feeling, while claiming victory over my situation.

Eventually, while holding on to God's grace, despite how it looked, what it felt like or what my mind was telling me, I was able to move closer to a safe zone. I knew that my mind was being attacked and that I could not continue this path. Everything was constantly in my head, the incident playing over and over again, and missing Edward seemed to appear more frequently. I found myself going back and forth, which only drove me harder in an effort to stand firm in knowing what the enemy was trying to do. I knew God would work it out for my good.

Waking up one morning, I could feel it. *Something appeared to be crushing me into bits inside and fear was showing up again.* I knew that I could not let fear hold me back; I needed to step into the light. The stronghold was more than I expected, the crushing stage was not my destiny, and it wasn't the end. I had to re-adjust and realize that there was something much bigger than my feelings. For those of you that are dealing with grief, just know, sometimes during the grieving stage, it's normal to want to release yourself from it all. As for me, knowing that no one will take care of the little ones as like myself, this readjustment began to motivate me; I began to see past Bernice. Most of the time, we are the ones who are in the way, but if we trust God more, we realize what we are going through is not the end. The enemy wants to keep us there, but I refused to allow fear to keep me from my final destiny. I was determined to find my breakthrough.

As an effort of getting away from it all, my family and I decided to take a road trip to Coronado in San Diego, California for the weekend. My daughter, whom was only six at the time, always watched my every move – she was so observant. She never questioned much as to what happened to dad. The school she was attending, Woodcrest Nazarene Christian School (WCNCS), was phenomenal and I am so grateful for her teachers, the staff and the pastor. As we drove to San Diego, I noticed two individuals in their car next to me - whom seemed to really be enjoying each other's company (I assumed they were in a relationship). As we continued to drive beside the vehicle - I began to feel sad. The tears began to roll down my face as I thought of all the times Edward and I drove to San Diego. My mind just went there - I *will never have this again.* I thought, *someone to love, to laugh with and enjoy everyday life.* As I looked into the rearview mirror - I noticed my daughter watching me. I felt some type of way because I had tried my best to not let my children see me in my low points. Quickly, I tried to pull myself together wiping the tears away as discreet as possible. All of a sudden, my daughter began to sing..."*How do you spell relief – J E S U S, How do you spell relief, J E S U S. J is for Jesus, E is for eternity, S is for Salvation and the rest is for US! How do you spell relief, J E S U S, how do you...*

Wow! As I listened - my daughter sang it again, and again. Immediately I started feeling like singing it with her. As we sang, I thought, *oh my God - my little angel.* To this day in her late 20s, she is still an amazing young woman and I wouldn't wish for anything more. This day will forever be with me. God's grace is phenomenal and when He shows up, it is always absolutely right on time. This moment reminded me of when my grandmother used to say, "Children are so innocent. You would be surprised what comes out of their mouths during difficult and challenging times." Yes, this was one of those out of the mouth of babes' moments.

When we are going through the many challenges called life, Satan is busy. He preys on our challenges, fears, failures and our mind-set, etc. He will get through any door that is left open. He prowls like a roaring lion seeking whom he can devour. I had to claim the victory with confidence in knowing who I am in Christ and remind the enemy that I'm no longer living in darkness, but reigning in the marvelous light of Jesus Christ. While keeping my eyes on Him, I also repented, asking God to forgive me for wanting to give up, wanting to die and feeling as though my life was over. I thought if I died (realizing now that I didn't really want to die) the children would be fine, someone would take care of them. Therefore, I had to learn how to balance my love for my children and my heartache. Losing someone you love - spouse, parents, children, sister, brother, and/or other close relationship - is a challenge and until you experience that type of loss, you don't understand the depth of its formality.

"I will go before you and make the crooked places straight"
(Isaiah 45:2a NKJV)

Living After Losing

Over My Circumstance – He Still Reigns

Living After Losing

Three months after Edward's death, while picking up my son (approximately three months old) from the babysitter, I noticed that he didn't seem his norm. He's usually a very happy baby but when I picked him up after work, he appeared different. Somewhat disoriented, the child-care assured me that he was fine and just awakening from a nap. Nevertheless, something still didn't seem quite right. After arriving home and attempting to change the baby, I noticed a very foul bowel movement with a red allergic reaction on his legs, stomach, etc. Quickly, I grabbed both my son and daughter and drove to the nearest hospital. I kept telling my daughter to keep him awake - for some reason, I was afraid that if he went to sleep, he wouldn't wake up. She and I began singing and talking to him; while driving, I would reach in the back to shake his little leg in an effort of keeping him awake.

We arrived at the emergency room and the triage nurse asked us to have a seat. Ten minutes went by and she still had not called us. Finally, after several attempts, we are escorted to a room in the back, but yet again, we are left in the room for more than 20 minutes. While at my son's bedside, I noticed he began to turn blue. I rushed out into the hallway, asked for his doctor - the lady I asked sarcastically stated, "I am the doctor". God knows, if I had been my 100% self...they would have had problems. I explained to her the change in my son's appearance and she then quickly moved into his room and stated, "He may be going into anaphylactic shock".

All of a sudden, I began to hear – "Code Pink to the emergency room! Respiratory to the emergency room!" Everyone was running around, and entered the room with my son. I thought I was going to lose my mind – I was asked to step out of the room; all I could remember is screaming out, "Lord, please don't take my son, too". I was devastated! A nun walked up to me and tried to comfort me. I tried to pull myself together and covered my mouth to de-escalate what my heart was really feeling. For the sake of my daughter, I tried hard to remain calm, but all I could think of was her peace of mind. While fighting to stay balanced, it took all I had. Shortly after my husband died, I remembered thinking how challenging it would be to care for two small children, "If only it was one child instead of two" and I allowed this thought to haunt me. I felt that maybe God was trying to get my attention to remind me that both children were a gift.

Shortly thereafter, a nun walked up to me asking, "Are you okay? Let me help you." I shook my head saying "No, I am not okay", and shared with her my thoughts about wishing there was only one child soon after Edward's death because of all the stress. The nun stated, "Oh no dear, God doesn't act in that way - it's understood, but no." She placed her arm around me and looked at me saying, "God would not punish you by taking away your son..." I needed to get out; I felt as though I was having an anxiety attack. Finally, I pulled myself together, took my daughter's hand and we walked towards the door. Outside the hospital, my daughter walked on the curb balancing herself while I held her hand and began silently praying.

After returning back to the emergency room, we saw that my mother and stepfather had arrived. The nurses escorted me to the back to visit with my son while my daughter stayed with my mom and dad. I kneeled next to the bed where my son laid with tubes connected everywhere. I began singing our favorite song. *"Jesus loves me, yes I know, for the Bible tells me so…"* The nurses watched me, little did I know, this was only the beginning.

My son had an allergic reaction; initially I was told it was anaphylactic shock, but praise God, it wasn't. Nevertheless, my son ended up in critical care for seven days due to the long wait to see the doctor and events that followed. After he was discharged, I was overwhelmed with family services and accusations of neglect due to the death of my husband. They thought that I had neglected my son due to the death of my husband! Never once was I asked about his daily activity with the babysitter before starting their case. I guessed later, after thinking it all over, the hospital needed to take the focus off of them. I was humiliated and unsure how to work it out. I remember calling my job, King/Drew Medical Center. Through the grace of God, at that time I was working with one of the chief physicians (Dr. Bala) who helped to keep my balance – thank you. He encouraged me that despite the rude behaviors, to nicely give social services anything they wanted because they could make my life very difficult. Therefore, despite the pressure, phone calls and the accusations, everything ended well. Thank you, Lord! I had no idea what I was up against but timing was everything. We don't realize why people are in our lives or our surroundings, but God always knows; He has already figured it out. This was true not just in this instance, but many other times also. He places people in our lives for a reason, for a season and some for a lifetime.

My mom was my rock. She was staying with me, helping to keep everything in order. God knows, this was a very busy and challenging time of my life. I would prepare breakfast for my six year old and drop her off to school, go to work, pick my daughter up from school, drop her back off at home to my mom and then prepare to spend the night at the hospital with my son. The next morning, the cycle repeated itself for about 10 days. My mom wasn't driving; this process lasted the entire time until my son was discharged. Keeping God in the center of my life was key; things would have been much more disruptive had I not. I believe that if I had been thinking properly, with less stress, I may have handled that situation quite differently with the hospital, but I was extremely thankful and my main concern at this time was my son and his health.

The thought of failing stayed in my head. Who would help me with my children as I try to stretch myself and provide for my family? How will I be able to provide...? All these thoughts were my battle. I knew that I could no longer fail; there was no room. I was all that I had. The devil was busy and fear was trying to take over my thoughts.

The plans that I had of graduating in two years with my graduate degree started to fade. I began to get comfortable with my current job and no longer sought for more. I knew that I was not totally in control of my life, but I was thankful.

For I knew that God develops our skills and gets us ready for what he has in store for our lives. At that moment, I decided to let go and turn it over to Him.

"Father, maximize my time in the word, continue to give me clear directions."

Living After Losing

Memories

Memories walk by our side, like a friend and comfort us. One year after Edward's dreadful death while preparing my morning for work and dropping the children off at their daily locations, I noticed a feeling of uneasiness. Everything seemed to be fine at first, but for some reason after arriving to work, I noticed a feeling of sadness and uncertainty. All I wanted at this time was to go back home and crawl into my bed. I tried to pinpoint what the problem was but couldn't think of anything that was causing these feelings. I was not depressed; everything at home was fine - the children, finances, my family, job, etc., but I still could not get a grip on it. This feeling went on for several days. I allowed the moment and accepted my feelings because after all, I was somewhat still there. After a week or so, things went back to normal and I began to feel better.

Our memories are our ability to recall past events. Memories are not meant to be depressing or make us feel as if life is pointless but rather give us a sense of peace. I did not quite understand this at the time, but the recollection of my memories of Edward made me realize the importance of planning for the children and our future. I began preparing and planning my will and burial so that it would not be a burden to my children. I also began wondering – if I would die today, who will take care of my children? I went as far as asking one of my sisters and a very dear friend of mine, "If anything were to happen to me, would you be willing to be the guardian for my children?" For some reason, I felt the need to ensure all bases were covered. I was afraid that my children would be left alone; it was important to me to ensure that it was understood "with whom they would be residing". Yes, we will all die at some point, but rather than dwell on that point – the way we live our lives is in our hands. We can determine how happy or successful we would like to be. I have realized that death has a way of putting life into perspective.

The following year, I started to experience the same exact feelings. "Why am I feeling this way?" Unsure of the sudden feelings, I continued my day, and finally realized that these feeling were leading again to that same day - January 30, 1998. I felt that my life was reliving this unfortunate cycle, this day will absolutely be a day I will never forget.

While thinking back, after purchasing my condo several years ago – escrow closed the same exact day - January 30th. Wow! Again, this was a heartbreaking reminder of this date. I am not sure how you feel about angels, but after Edward died, I always felt "yet another angel is in heaven watching down on his family". This was unquestionably one of the only ways that I was able to move on. I believe that one day, we will see our loved ones again and the very thought of knowing that this is not the end gave me hope.

BECOMING – Through several trials, I learned how to handle these feeling differently. For the upcoming years, I decided to evaluate/analyze these feelings. I wanted to understand more as to why I was feeling this way. Why does my heart ache as if it was yesterday? So many questions. True enough, the feelings resurfacing around this date became a ritual. While understanding the on-set of my feelings of uncertainty - instead of reacting to the negative feelings, I focused on understanding where my emotions were coming from. I noticed that they were the days Edward and I celebrated together - holidays, birthdays, Father's Day, etc. - these days our families would get together and love each other, cook, play music and games, etc., but these days were no longer a part of my annual rituals - they became hard days for me, I felt lonely, sad and missed him more. While adjusting to the NEW norm, I began to realize that although Edward was no longer here with us - family was still important. I'm not sure how this all works, but I do know that every year before I got a grasp on it, I was unable to quickly accept life on its terms and move forward.

I can still see Edward kneeling at the side of my daughter's bed exactly where I found him. During my darkest moments, there were also moments of light - the memories and things that still remained of his life i.e., our children, his son Donovan, his siblings and the time we spent together - all of which was left behind. I wanted to hold on to those memories and part of me wanted them to materialize. After all, memories are all we have left; I had an immeasurable desire to tell anyone who would listen to the moments I could remember spending with him. Yes, I wanted to hold on. Memories allow our loved ones to continue to live after they are gone. We hold on to their belongings, objects and yes, moments that remind us of them. Thank God for memories!

Life is simple, but all the hassle, the stressors and issues that we incur in our daily lives eventually catches up with us and throw us off guard. Remember, absolutely everything happens exactly at the right time regardless if we think it's too late or too soon. The Bible says, *"Let us boldly approach the throne of our gracious God, where we may receive mercy and his grace to find timely help" (Hebrews 4:16 NEB).* I know that when we accept the fact that God is in control of our lives, we can better accept becoming who we are meant to be. Becoming in both our personal life as well as our professional lives **TIMELY.** Not too soon, not too late. Just on time. Time is very important here because, everything is done at certain moments in our lives. We may not always understand the timing, but trust me, time waits on no one and often, it is surprisingly unexpected. Our journey is already planned, and it may take some of us longer to get there because of our own personal choices, but eventually we will all get there.

There are certain mountains only God can climb, and it is not that we are not welcome to try, we just are not able. If we would be still – and take a different approach the outcome would be grand. Think about the children in the book of Exodus – It took Moses 40 days and 40 nights to bring the Israelites out of the wilderness. This was not God's initial plan for their life, but because of the constant murmuring and not trusting God, the trip took longer than expected. There have been many times I wanted to pursue something, but because my mind was made up to do it my way – I procrastinated and wasted time. For instance, after my husband died – I wanted to hold on to Edward, it was hard for me to let go, and since it was difficult for me to leave that dark place – the healing process took longer. Yes, being conscious of our emotional time clock is important! Understanding that this too shall pass is inevitable – because what we are telling ourselves is, "I do not have to stay here".

Dissatisfaction also plays a major role in our sadness. It often keeps us from doing the things we want. I noticed, once I started practicing gratitude, I re-framed my perception of what is now. Being grateful for the here and now, even in the absence of the very thing we desire. "Faith is not what we see...." We do have choices and we can choose to be happy. Being content with life stems from our feelings and being in charge of our very own lives. Contentment equally allows us time, to embrace the struggle, and keep us on the right path. While I pray that at least some portion of what I learned from my most challenging experiences is reflected on these pages, it will allow you to also see the brighter side of it all. May love and cherished memories, always bring comfort to you as you become the best version of yourself.

"May our Lord Jesus Christ himself and God our Father
encourage you and strengthen you
in every good thing you do and say."
(2 Thessalonians 2:16)

Living After Losing

Stepping into the Light

Living After Losing

My first NEW step, was to start back going to church regularly. TBN and all the magnificent speakers were wonderful, but my fellowship was lacking. My first Sunday going back, as I was sitting there listening, I felt as though the pastor was speaking directly to me. I felt that he knew my story because he seemed to have hit every angle as if he was reading it out loud. I became distracted, feeling that my story had been discussed, but instead of focusing on this small detail, I continued to listen. By no surprise, at the end of the service, I went down for the altar call. While talking to the pastor about my recent loss, I no longer could hold it in. Uncontrollably, I began to let out this cry: "*Oh my God!* "He began to pray for me... I continued to call out to God. The church members began to take the baby from my arms and my young daughter while taking me to the back where I remained for a couple of hours. This was actually the moment that I started truly feeling some type of relief. I felt as though the pain and everything else that I was holding on the inside came out. I knew that this was only the beginning and more was needed; I continued to go to seek God's face and endure His presence.

The following Sunday, I began going to church regularly, the pastor, first lady and congregation treated us like family. After that rewarding experience, I had to ask my friend if she had told the Pastor my story. She denied it. Maybe she did or maybe no; it really didn't matter much anymore because that day was the beginning of a NEW me. My thoughts and my hunger for more was the beginning of getting it right.

Eventually, I joined my dear friend DL's church and it was the most amazing beginning. I re-dedicated my life to Christ; started counseling with the pastor and started my new walk with an assurance that God is with me and He will never leave my side. My pastor at this time re-assured me that I could not blame myself for Edward's death and his need of being in denial. It still took me awhile before I finally let go of the guilt, wishing that I knew he was in trouble.

During counseling with the pastor, he offered me a position as a Grievance Counselor, so I could share my story, my walk and some of my experiences. I had received my graduate degree and he thought working in the church would be a good start for me. He wanted me to start a class at the church on grieving to help myself as well as others on this new journey; however, I felt so broken. How could I be a service to others when I could barely minister to myself? The pastor tried to convince me that through ministering and God's guidance, I would be fine, but at that time I wasn't ready. I knew that I wasn't strong enough; I would cry even when someone would just mention my loss to me... Little did I know, it wasn't about my fear, nor what I felt; it was about Him.

As time passed, I started trying to live once again, through counseling, my children, memories of Edward, family, friends and my TBN family. Reality began to set in, justifying that when we are tempted, God will provide a way out of no way, so that we can stand up under it. No longer did I wait for someone to wake me from my dream. I began appreciating who I was in Christ and being thankful for all the doors that God had opened - the opportunities, the vision of writing my book, starting my own business and the many steps that I still have not completely taken. Knowing that God provides was my safe place. The doors that I was afraid of, He carried me through them all - thank you, Lord!

I was on FIRE! This was definitely what I needed - to get me stirred up. I began to listen more to my tapes, TBN, my pastor, sharing my testimonies, etc. I knew God was working in my life. New doors of opportunity started opening both at work and in my spiritual walk.

Fast forward to 2016 - the first lady of the church at my children's Christian school telephoned me out of nowhere and asked if I could speak on Mother's Day at the Church. I was honored, and at the same time, a little uncomfortable considering I had never spoken in front of a church congregation with so many people. My heart told me to go on, do not turn down the invitation. Although, I was nervous, I accepted the invitation.

By mid-week, I began to ponder. What should I say in front of the congregation? I didn't think my story would be adequate; therefore, anxiety and fear began to set in. Although, I knew that fear comes with our emotional rollercoaster when God is trying to stretch us, I pressed forward trying to figure out what I should say. How I will get myself to a certain level in order to speak to the entire congregation on Mother's Day? Why me I questioned? I clearly heard "Why not?" My mind began to race, this would be my very first time speaking in front of an entire congregation; the first time, I would share my story publicly with a group of people. Was this God requiring maturity, demanding that I stop hiding? I started preparing my testimony for Mother's Day. Although, my heart still felt heavy, I pressed forward. The next day, my eldest sister stopped by. As we spoke, I mentioned the invitation to her since she had spoken in church several times and I knew she could tell me something to help relieve my tension. After sharing the excitement of being honored that I had been asked, at the same time my feelings of nervousness while trying to implement the plan was overwhelming. I asked her, "What should I say or speak about?" After listening for a while, my sister told me, "Know this is not really about you". I thought about what she said - it is not about me. She went on to say, "It's about Him and once you realize it's about Him it gets easier". Yes! It was absolutely about Him. Ultimately the victory we seek is not ours; the victory is God's. He uses us to give Him the victory.

Later that day, music began to play lightly in my head; I began to hear a light sound with the music sounding like a trumpet playing. I tried to adjust the sound by rubbing my ears. The sound begin to increase was so beautiful, a sound that was not familiar, but a beautiful sound. I began to embrace the sound: the feelings of anxiety and trying to figure out what had seemed to be an issue, was no longer an issue. My sister was right! The trumpets…The information I already had - I'm absolutely sure, the Holy Spirit was directing me as he had been doing all along. I thanked God for his Mercy and Grace which allows me to share my journey to let people know how amazing He is.

I was confident that Sunday would be a good day. I thought about Joshua when the Israelites were in battle with the Amalekites in Exodus 17:8. As long as Moses held up his hands, the Israelites were winning. When he lowered his hands, they would lose so, Aaron and Hur sat on both sides in an effort to keep his arms up which is how they defeated the Amalekites. I truly believe God's Word because sometimes, some of us think we are winning on our own. My interpretation of this story is the Israelites thought they were winning, but didn't realize they were winning when Moses was holding up the staff of God in his hands. I was further enlightened while thinking of the passage "Footsteps". As I look back, I knew God had carried me. I needed to use that same strategy on Mother's Day and every day throughout my life. I will speak from my heart and give my testimony on how wonderful God is.

I continued to spend more time with God. I began praying and asking God to maximize my time in the word to give me clear directions. Our God is a strategic God who will use our situations to give us a fresh start, a fresh opportunity. So, I began to "stir it up". That Sunday was amazing. I have to admit, my planned speech was prepared; I knew exactly what I would say and how the speech would be delivered. But, God had another plan. When I went up, a little nervous, my prepared speech was never spoken. I began to speak a thing from my heart by sharing my initial walk through losing someone I deeply loved. I have to admit, I teared up a little, but it was absolutely great!

I felt really good after sharing my story. My support system, daughter (Jade), son (Justin) and close co-worker (Kim) were all there in support. I truly wanted to end my testimony with how God had delivered me from a very dark place. I also wanted to share where the end of the road has taken me today. In terms of my daughter, who graduated from Howard University with a major in Biology, she is focused on being an anesthesiologist and is studying to take the MCAT for medical school. My son, who is currently attending UCLA with a major in Biology, has a passion to become a heart surgeon. Wow! Look at God! Although, my prayers to God were always about my children and their well-being, He never failed and I am so very thankful. Ending my testimony this way was not the plan because it wasn't about me or the children at this time - it was about Him. Praise the all-living God!

After the service, a few women came up to me saying my testimony really hit home for them. Some enjoyed my testimony because they, too, had lost their husbands. My testimony was "my truth" and giving God the praise for his amazing Grace is my beginning and my end. Thank you, Father!

REAPING WHAT YOU'VE SOWN - I vividly remember, women coming up to me at my job several months after returning to work when my husband died saying, "Oh, my God, you helped me so much". I was totally flabbergasted at their accusations; I had no idea such an impact was left on these women's lives during my time of grieving. I was so broken; how could I have left an impressive impact on so many? A few would tell me, "You don't remember, but you told me *this*, or you told me *that*". During one conversation, a young lady mentioned that I expressed the importance of appreciating their husbands because once he is gone, there are no second chances. She thanked me and told me that I helped to save her marriage. Isn't it wonderful how God uses us in time of need for someone and we have no idea that through Him, our words are literally helping them?

As these memories were brought to my attention, they made me feel a certain kind of way. I continued to write a little, procrastinate, doing this or the other. So much time was wasted, and maybe, that was the plan. Yet, I do believe He prepares us for the journey that He has for us and even when we feel as though we missed it, God is still always on time.

After several years, things had gotten a lot better. I have to admit that when it comes to stepping into the light, I am not the most accepting when it comes to moving quickly. By all means, I have learned over the past years that we cannot expect change by stagnation. Everyone without a doubt goes through tremendous change and have difficulty getting back, yet some of us seem to embrace it better than others.

"Your word is a lamp to guide my feet and a light for my path."
(Psalms 119:105 NLT)

Making a Real Impact

Dare to Live

I began sharing my story whenever the opportunity arose. Situations where I was uncomfortable became some of the most amazing experiences for me. I began to get a sense of relief which forced me to share my testimony more and it started to feel like therapy. Over a period of time, I would find myself in conversations that eventually ended up with me sharing my testimony, which in return seemed to have been good for both myself as well as the individual. Also, there have been situations where I was battling or having a not so good day, and I was still able to hold myself up while at the same time, comforting someone else. Isn't this how our Father works? Doesn't He always show up at the right time when we least expect it?

I was continued steered back to the book - I began to think that maybe it was time for me to stop putting off what God gave me years ago - to share my story. Initially, there was so much pain and whenever I spoke of Edward, I would just break down and cry. I couldn't share my story, not now. Then I began to think, maybe it was too late. The enemy still tried to remain in my thoughts reminding me that it was too late since God had given me that vision and I didn't move forward. Needless to say, although the book was not written, subconsciously I was still sharing my story every chance I got.

As my heart healed, I was able to talk about the loss of my husband without falling apart. I began listening to other women's stories and finding out how our stories were very similar. I decided to ask questions; I interviewed based on losing people and the things we love. Many of their stories and feelings saddened me because I knew all too well the patterns when experiencing loss. Regardless of the loss we struggle with, finding peace and acceptance is of the utmost importance. We all have our own patterns when it comes to handling life situations, but once we start walking in alignment with God, we start seeing things different.

One of my discussions was with a co-worker who was going through a separation/divorce with her husband and was having a very difficult time. Initially, I believed that, when losing a loved one from death, it had to be more devastating than losing from divorce or separation. However, I learned something that day through our many conversations. This young lady was having a very difficult time, too, and she still loved her husband very much. I learned that her feelings were very similar to those of my very own. After her husband decided to take a different route that ended in a divorce, she was devastated. Her feelings of hurt, abandonment, betrayal, loneliness, and most of all disbelief, had her in a place that was all so familiar. She loved her husband so much, was not in agreement with the divorce and was depressed from the separation which she felt was a loss after 10 years of marriage.

After interviewing a few other women, I also learned that these women had mixed emotions. They felt that losing a loved one through death seemed to be easier because he's no longer here. Death is then considered the end of the chapter and although they would miss him or her, that person is infinitely gone. They equally felt that there would be no worries about whom he or she is dating. The relationship is over and that particular person is no longer in your life. But on the other hand, I feel that although I'm no longer with my husband through divorce, he is still here. He is still breathing and carrying on with his life here on earth. His family still have him and so do the children. Although, he and I couldn't make it, he is still here and can continue to play major roles in the lives of people who love him. I guess there are mixed emotions on this topic but, all in all - either way we both are losing and from my understanding, the loss is still inevitable.

Have you ever felt like going around, under and above a situation? Have you ever felt like Lord, I can't go through this - not now, Lord? After this conversation, I realized that although her husband was not dead, with the loss that she and I both were experiencing, the bottom line was that we both hurt from the loss. Yes, although her husband was still here on earth, the feelings of abandonment, devastation, hurt, anger and loneliness were still the same. This was absolutely the day I concluded, although circumstances are different and in some ways they are very similar, a loss is simply a loss despite it all.

It doesn't matter what our personal situation is at this time, grieving and feelings of abandonment have the same end results when losing what we love. Many of us who may not have experienced loss, do not really understand the struggle. It's hard on the outside, because what's inside has to be protected from the whispers, stares, disappointments, heartaches, rumors and opinions of others. People always seem to have an opinion and most of the time, have no idea of the circumstances. I believe when you experience losing someone from death, this experience outcasts anything else that you will ever experience. There is absolutely nothing that can hurt more – the small things in life that seem to overwhelm so many, is only a fraction of what can really get your attention and catch you off guard.

"He shall be like a tree planted by the rivers…"
(Psalm 1:3a NKJV)

Losing is Losing

Dare to Live

Loss is as much a part of human existence as breathing. It is an everyday event - a lost cell phone, Apple Airpod earphones, a wallet, keys, earrings, investment opportunities, your dog, a relationship. In most cases, we ponder what may have been, get frustrated and eventually move on. But when these losses can't be shrugged off, it eventually triggers a different type of emotional response as like when someone broke into my home on December 23, 2016. It was two days before Christmas. I will never forget...my daughter was coming home for winter break. I picked her up from the airport and returned home. We didn't notice right away, but soon thereafter, we noticed missing items from the home - televisions, electronics, clothing, bags, etc. Someone had broken into our home and had taken more than $15,000 worth of our personal belongings. We were gone less than 45 minutes.

Chances are, you have experienced something very similar. Maybe, you have lost a job, a beloved pet, loss of a loved one, your marriage ended in divorce or maybe your health by a chronic illness. Each individual loss, regardless of the loss, has its own personal and private experience. The way we respond to a loss is determined by multiple factors. Nevertheless, just as there are common patterns to being violated or experienced during loss, there are also common responses that will eventually be encountered at some point in time. For example, when I experienced someone breaking into my home two days before Christmas, I was devastated, but at the same time felt like being in control was more important, not only for me, but for my son and daughter.

Two days before Christmas! This is absolutely, one of my favorite holidays. Literally, I was in an emotional state, feeling numb, and a sense of hopelessness. I guess it could be interpreted as my front line defense against the overwhelming reality that someone had broken into my home and taken our personal belongings - items that were very dear to us.

Feelings of insecurity sets in whenever a loss suddenly changes the course of our lives. Breaking the line from the past that we cherished to the future we counted on, the complex feelings that may be experienced are considered grief. Most of us know that grief is not a standard; we don't go in thinking that it will be a certain way. All of our actions will differ from one to the other with every loss we experience. When going through different types of losses, we have to be able to stop and keep God in the center no matter what. Otherwise, our situation does not get better; the challenge becomes more challenging. The key is to be transformed, with a new mindset, and it doesn't happen instantly - it takes time. There will be a time to grieve and adjust to our new life and yes, *time does heal wounds*.

I have learned to pray more when challenges arrive, and believe that God is still alive. Feelings of loss and grief are natural responses when we experience the loss of our possessions, our health, freedom and the people we love. We are all thrown off balance when we lose the things we love and care about. We tend to spend time and time again trying to figure this thing out. It may be easy for me to say this now since I've gone through many losses; prayer does save time;

it beats going in circles just to come back to the same center. It's perfectly fine to have your moment - but by all means, don't stay there. If we trust God, the challenge is no longer a challenge. The loss is still a loss, but through our trust in Him we are able to surpass all the unnecessary worries and all the complicated questions. We can have peace by knowing that God has us.

Generally, when losing there are *seven stages of grief*[1] *(disbelief, anger, denial, guilt, depression, bargaining, and acceptance)*, and each step differs from the other. I believe, the stages of loss is based on the loss that is being experienced. For instance, my experience with **Denial** and **Disbelief** was the first step after losing my husband and for some reason, I did not want to believe that Edward was gone. I kept waiting for him to walk in the door or for me to wake up - I was in disbelief. I was having difficulty accepting the loss and it allowed me to stay there longer than I wanted. However, when someone broke into my home, it was **Anger** and a different type of **Disbelief** that set in, I was so angry that someone had literally violated my family, and my home in this type of way. My thoughts were so out of control.

We work so hard for our possessions, and for someone to just walk into our lives and take them from us is outrageous. How is this possible? Having to deal with this type of loss was much more than I wanted to deal with. But rather stay there, through prayer – I was able to let it go. Rather than focus on the loss, I focused more on being thankful that my children nor myself was home during the break in. I could have gone into a deep **Depression** considering the loss (more than $15,000) but, quickly accepted the loss and moved forward. This stage is absolutely a stage where you do not want to stay long. On the other hand, while dealing with depression when my husband died, it was so easy for me to stay there - the experience allowed me to feel some sort of way and I did not want to accept my loss nor move on. My experience with **Guilt** forced me into counseling. I felt that I should have known, maybe by ensuring my husband was taking his medication. Through therapy, I had to realize that Edward was in charge of his own life. Nevertheless, I still couldn't get past - maybe if I had handled things differently...

After my home was invaded, guilt set in once again. Maybe if I had got the alarm on the house earlier…maybe if I didn't trust my neighbors…or the neighborhood, maybe… Finally, you have to get to the point where you realize things happen. The worst thing to do is blame yourself. **Acceptance** seemed to be the last stage for me. Although, the journey seemed so long, once you reach this stage everything is up hill. From my experience, you cannot compare the loss of an individual with the loss of some type of possession. Once I accepted each of my losses, it was noticeable how fast I was able to move forward? We have to allow ourselves to get at a stage of self-resilience - acceptance and allow ourselves to begin to live past the grief. We may not all experience all seven stages, but I am absolutely certain that, we will have some experience with at least three of the stages. Through my personal experience, I absolutely do not remember **bargaining;** however, denial, guilt, anger, depression and finally acceptance played major roles.

Another very important category that will help you get past the devastating feeling of losing is having faith. **Faith** - is what we believe. Nevertheless, believing is one thing, but actually believing outside of our five (5) senses - *sight, hear, touch, smell and taste* - takes faith and actually trusting God. Trusting God during the devastating losses in your life and afterwards truly will transform your life. I began learning to keep Him in the center of it all. I wished at this time - I understood faith the way I understand it today. If so, I wouldn't have been so far off - I would be simply amazing!

Every stage of life has its own storms, tests, losses and gains. When God opens a door He has already equipped us with the tools we need to succeed. Being able to feel, and resist is key to keeping control of our circumstances. I struggled every day to find a way to keep going - what do you think you would do at a time of loss? What have you done? I've learned not to carry my burdens, nor my mistakes around with me. Instead, I've learned to place them under my feet and use them as stepping stones to rise above them while keeping me balanced and faithful.

"Now faith is the substance of things hoped for,
the evidence of things not seen."
(Hebrews 11:1 NKJV)

End Note

1. https://www.healthline.com/health/stages-of-grief

There is a Chance

Dare to Live

Through what seem to be an endless road, "my truth" came to light. I had to realize that despite it all, if nothing else, I had to live for my children and to my very best be all that I could for them both. Prayer became the interval part of my life. No longer did I feel alone, nor had the pity parties that came with the grieving process. No longer did I want to die! I began to thank God for the wonderful time He allowed me and Edward to share and the beautiful children that He blessed us with together. I thanked Him for His mercy, for his Grace and for loving us. I thanked God for his faithfulness and the Holy Spirit, my teacher, for forever being the light to my path. No longer did I feel my life was incomplete.

Sometimes when in this process of loss we tend to focus on the loss and not the lesson. I believe that during each of our trials, there is something we must endure and something learned. While in the midst of the storm, staying focused on the truth (what God has said) will always get you through. Like Joyce Meyer says, "Enjoy where you are on the way to where you're going." But, how could we enjoy such a heartfelt situation such as death, loss, sickness, pain, depression, divorce, etc.? Simply by keeping God in the center of it all. As for myself, it wasn't easy, but through my journey, I've learned and the three of us survived. We prevailed! I realized, there was absolutely no one in this world that would BETTER love my children nor take care of them than myself. Yes, there is a chance!

Begin by understanding that your mouth is a powerful weapon; began to speak it into existence. Start confessing that you shall have whatever you want, and the power of life and death lie in your tongue (Proverbs 18:21). Also, enter into your season of celebration, rejoicing and thanksgiving. You, too can put your past behind. Your former years of hardship, sickness, tears, brokenness, depression, stagnation, and lack are over. God has turned your situation around into something NEW.

Looking further back, do not reflect on other people's opinions and their advice as to where they think you should be or how long to grieve, but through God's grace, you will begin to handle situations differently. I no longer reacted to people's personal opinions or allowed what they thought to define me. Most people have no idea what you are going through. They are only trying to help, but "Until, you absolutely experience loss, you have no idea what it feels like". People are so quick to say, "I understand or I know how you feel". I think not, especially if you have not gone through the challenge of losing something or someone that is so very dear to you. We have to step outside of our comfort zone and learn how to live, by first realizing that God has not given up on you. There is a chance.

Everyone handles loss differently and what may be small to me, may be large for the next person. Often, I had to remind myself that although my circumstances were devastating, remembering not to become the judge of anyone else's life situation is of utmost importance. At the end of the day, it's not about the challenge, circumstance or the trial, it's about the way we handle it. Regardless to what it looks like, how it feels or what is being said, our reaction is still the bottom-line.

Over the past years, I have been focusing more on God constantly, asking Him to teach me to be more like Him. Only God can give us what we need. Today, I'm no longer living in fear - no longer holding on to my circumstances nor fearful of being alone. It's time and now is the best time ever!

"But seek ye first the Kingdom of God, and His righteousness; and all these things shall be added unto you."
(Matthew 6:33 KJV)

Dare to Live

The Only Opinion That Matters

I have learned over the past few years that it is not the circumstances that keep us down, it's how we process it. Whether we are processing the loss of something taken from us, our homes, the loss from an unexpected illness or death of a loved one. Be aware of the opinions and feelings that we experience. We can easily begin to feel that we are not enough, our life will never be fulfilled or disconnecting ourselves from people we love. These types of acts will only keep us in this rut.

There was a time when I would leave the house - whether it was grocery shopping or just to get out and as I drove, I would see a significant amount of people enjoying each other's company. I noticed what appeared to be a husband, wife and family driving by enjoying family outings. It made me feel so alone; I felt totally disconnected. I thought, no longer would I have these essential pleasures of what society called family. These thoughts, as well as the thought of my children growing up without their dad, made me feel so incomplete. My son will never have the experience of knowing what it was like to have his dad in his life, someone to help him grow into a mature, effective young man. My daughter would never hear her dad tell her how remarkable and beautiful she was. These thoughts seemed to control my thought processes; I couldn't think of anything but the loss I had experienced and what I no longer had that would make me feel complete.

It frightened me more and more as I thought of being a single parent. How would I provide for my family with only a bachelor's degree? How would I give my children the love they needed from both their parents, especially my son? I figured it would be easy to teach my daughter how to be a lady, but how would I teach my son to be a loving and supportive young man and a father? I allowed this and other questions about me remarrying make me feel some type of way, as though I was missing something to be complete.

I began to lift myself up spiritually. I proclaimed God's promise in my life. Satan cannot take what Jesus had already given to me. I decided to go back to a familiar church family where the Pastor focused on the Word, teaching us how to fight our battles; to declare and decree what Grace has already given to us when he died on the Cross. Jesus has already paid the price and I believe He cannot do what my faith cannot carry. I have learned how to pray, how to stand firm on God's word by standing my ground and not settling for less - go for the full price! Yes, Jesus paid and has paid the full price. I am enough!

Lord, teach me to be more like You, Father God. Build me up, help me to stay balanced and not allow the things of the world to distract me. I know it is impossible to have what my faith cannot carry. I declare and I decree to guard my life with the truth of Your word. Thank you, Lord, in Jesus name, Amen.

"He that hath ears to hear, let him hear."
(Matthew 13:9 KJV)

Fearfully Made

When dealing with a loss, understand that fear makes our problems appear much bigger than they are. These include the fear of not having enough, the fear of not being able to replace what was taken, and the fear of being alone, etc. Maybe that obstacle that felt permanent was really only temporary. What if we change our mind-set and see our obstacle as just a challenge? Once we go through that door, we may possibly realize it is not as big as we thought it was. Now, how do you begin to get in sync with the reality of what frightens us most when we are alone and grief stricken? Fear and anxiety can last for as long as we make it possible. If we are not careful, we can get stuck with them. In some cases, they can take over our lives, affecting our ability to eat, sleep, concentrate, leave our homes or simply enjoy life. During my losses, I didn't quite understand how amazing life can be despite it all when we take our eyes off our situations...when we focus less on our ability and more on Him. What do you do when you don't know what to do?

I tried to think of scriptures that would help bring me out of my dark place. These scriptures came to mind: *"Behold, I send an Angel before thee, to keep thee in the way, and to bring thee into a place which I have prepared"* (Exodus 23:20 KJV). *"My flesh and heart fail, but God is the strength of my heart, and my portion forever"* (Psalm 73:26 NKJV). *"I sought the Lord, and He heard me, and delivered me from all my fears" (Psalms 34:4 NKJV).* No weapon formed against me will prevail (based on Isaiah 54:17a NIV). But what I didn't know at this time was that my fear presented itself much bigger than it truly was. FEELINGS - I allowed my feelings to get in the way; faith is not about what it feels like, but I knew that. Nevertheless, when we are so distraught, we feel overwhelmed. During our distress, we become vulnerable and leave the door open (this is how the enemy gets in). Although, I knew better - I continued to give time to my thoughts of fear. Instead of answering back with faith, I allowed my fear to take control. All the lessons I had learned over the years went out the window.

What happened to "guarding your mind"? Why was it so hard for me to accept the fact that nothing is promised to us? God can send us instruction, wisdom, and provision, but we miss it because we are not paying attention. I realized, He does giveth and He taketh away. Maybe we will have some challenges and disappointments, but the bottom line, whatever the situation is, we must learn to trust God more. Joyce Meyer says, "You can't move forward constantly looking out the rearview mirror".

Life doesn't happen to us, we happen to life. Fear is one of our most powerful emotions. It has a very strong effect on our body and mind. Do not let your thoughts run away from you. The enemy knows our weaknesses – this is the time that he takes advantage and prowls around like a lion in an effort to kill, steal and destroy! Control your thought processes. It's perfectly fine to grieve; to miss the people and the things that we love. But, it is equally important to cope with fear so that it does not stop you from living.

"I praise You because I am fearfully and wonderfully made; Your works are wonderful, I know that full well."
(Psalm 139:14 NIV)

Adjusting My Crown

I will never forget the message I heard one evening, while listening to Bishop T.D. Jakes. He spoke on "Taking control of your life". I remember him saying, "*You know why most people are depressed? Most folks are depressed because they want to be depressed. Either they want to change something they cannot change or they want something they cannot have*". Yikes!! That's me I thought! Literally, I would sit in my bed with my eyes affixed to one corner of my bedroom for hours wishing that Edward would come home, that I would awaken and this would all be a dream.

Thinking back quickly at my Mom's accusations while staying at my house a few days after Edward died. She said, "She heard someone knock on the door; she asked, "Who is it?" to which there was no answer. She opened the door and no one was there. Again...knock, knock. Mom asked, "Who's there?" No answer again. She checks and no one is there. Mom thought it to be strange as our complex only had 10 condos and it would be very easy to see someone. Mom believed that it was Edward. She stated he wasn't ready... Well, I surely wasn't ready either. Now as I think back, maybe subconsciously, I waited... Nevertheless, after hearing T.D. Jake's sermon, I asked myself, why do you sit here waiting for something that will never happen? Yes! It was time to adjust my crown. This message was absolutely for me and it was time to move forward!

Listening to T.D. Jakes was the beginning of many breakthroughs and although TBN was a blessing, I still needed more. I needed God and the power of deliverance to help bring me through this place. The more I listened, the more I yearned. Realizing that I needed fellowship, I was ready to surrender my all and I became even more desperate for Him. Constantly, I began to ask God to teach me how to be more like Him - I wanted to know Him more. Speak to me now, Lord! Only You can give me what I need.

Today, when I think about the phrase "Get *Ready. Stay Ready!*" I realize that I am ready, no longer living in fear, and no longer holding onto circumstances nor feelings of insecurities. I am thankful and hopeful for the Glory of God. "Father God, Your word in 2 Timothy 1:7 KJV *For God hath not given us the spirit of fear; but of power, and love and of a sound mind.* Father, help me to be a light to my path of darkness. Teach me. Show me, Father, how to let go of my fear. It had been long enough and it was time to depart and let go. It was time to stand on the Word and know that God giveth and he taketh away. Grace, grace, all is well – CROWN ADJUSTED.

"Trust in the Lord with all thine heart;
and lean not unto thine own understanding."
(Proverbs 3:5 KJV)

Self-Care:
Cultivating New Habits

Eventually coming to terms with self and addressing our emotional struggles is something we all will face at some point in time. I knew without a doubt that the personal struggles I have endured during my losses provided insight that I could not have had otherwise. Once I learned to live, I accepted that sometimes our plans and goals are not that of God.

Some really good tips that were able to help me was cultivating new habits for self-care. I've learned how to focus on what can be done and what cannot be done. Beyond that meant grappling with whatever you are struggling with, accept the loss and eventually you will see what is far most important.

Several years ago, while supporting a friend who was battling with drugs, I knew nothing about being an enabler. That day, after listening to all who had spoken – I realized that I was an enabler, and I was not helping her the way she needed help. I was literally one of her enablers. Wow! That taught me to help her, not by her terms, but in a healthy and drug-free approach.

This was also the day that I learned their "Serenity Prayer" - To accept the things I cannot change and to change the things I can. Still today, I would find myself analyzing my situations, asking "Is this something I can change?" If so, I make plans to change it and if not, I must move on quickly.

Finally, realizing that God was working through me - as time continued to pass, I accepted the fact that Edward and everything else I had loss were gone and began to focus on my mental, emotional and physical health. Although it's simple, at times we get caught up in our fast-paced lifestyles that often overlook the importance of our mental and physical health. My life has changed and I can finally find my true balance. I started working towards improving my mood, reducing my anxiety and finding ways to live after losing. This focus allowed me to readjust my thoughts, to stand firm and take one day at a time. This really began to work for me.

Sometimes we get caught up in all the things going on around us - feelings of fear, loneliness, and depression - that we forget that God has worked it out while we were trying to figure it out. Now that I see how God was working in me, I realize there was a stronghold on me during the multiple challenges I faced. My desire to "dare and live" through it all has allowed me to see the importance of taking time out for me and incorporating self-care as an interval part of this puzzle. It was time for me and now, it's time for you to cultivate NEW habits. Taking your thoughts captive and ensuring your mental health is intact – this is an excellent start for self-cultivating.

I truly believe that we can control our thoughts and our destiny by taking control of our situation. We all have a choice to a balance life when things are good and not so good. No one and no circumstance can ever take that away from us - we have the right to choose to be happy, and to choose to be free!

Let's start by finding more time for family and friends. Workout and start a plan that will mentally get you fit. Most importantly, know in your heart that the challenge of life is just as important as the good things and through each challenge, you will prevail. We must have an attitude of hope. Yesterday ended last night and today is a NEW day.

In a robust way, identify ways to develop healthy habits. Here's a guide to get you started, you may use this guide by adding or deleting to help cultivate your own positive habits:

- Develop a positive mental attitude
- Set goals and focus
- Exercise and choose healthy eating choices
- Create sources of motivation or inspiration
- Track your progress

"Incremental change is better than ambitious failure"
~ Tony Schwartz

Dare to Live

Importance of Support

Support during this time is of the utmost importance. Having a support system has many positive benefits, such as better coping skills, a healthier life and higher levels of wellbeing. As mentioned earlier, support does help to reduce depression and anxiety, but family and friends may not always know how to be supportive - this is one reason why self-care is important. Sometimes families and friends may want to be there, but don't know how.

My support system was very low during my time of grieving. There may have been three individuals from my husband's family that kept in touch for a little while after Edward died, but as time went on, there was no one. This made me feel bad because I felt that his family was my family; they treated me as though we were family but as soon as Edward died, so did we. My family on the other hand, of course was there - they tried very hard, but I'm not sure they really knew how. I believe that they didn't want to see me in this dark place, they would try to encourage me to meet someone. I knew their intentions were good, but they truly did not understand that I really wasn't ready...

During our initial stage of grieving - we feel trapped and unsure as to moving forward. No one seems to understand where we are coming from nor do they understand the loss that we are experiencing. It's easy for one to start distancing themselves from everyone, the family outings, friends, etc. These are feelings that we must learn how to deal with and not run away from. I suggest that when feeling overwhelmed, stop and try to take control of these feelings.

It's not always easy, but at least try to control the way you react. You have the power to have whatever you want, so why not take charge of this situation? Take charge of your life!

Today, when I look at my children and myself in the mirror, I can't imagine how lost I was. I'm thankful for all the doors and the guidance that help me to get out of that dark place. I've experienced darkness in several situations, but death was the hardest yet. I never want anyone to have to experience such turmoil, loneliness, fear, depression, disconnect and pain. I want men and women to know that when losing a loved one, getting bad news from the doctor, losing a body part, getting a divorce, relationship gone bad or just simply being violated - it absolutely is not the end. Accept the loss and try to focus more on your healing of acceptance and moving forward. Time absolutely does heal all wounds.

Each and every one of us will someday die and go towards the journey that God has for us after life here on earth. But, when we do, those that are left behind will experience a loss, a separation they haven't known. Losing people we love is absolutely not a good feeling. But, when you know Jesus, the pain is lighter. When you know Jesus, what seems like a battle will become a challenge, but yet a challenge that will lift your spirits and keep you going! A challenge that made me decide that together, He and I can do this because long as I keep my eyes on God, all things are possible.

Today, I continue to allow God to direct my footsteps by using my eyes to see and my ears to hear. It was far past time for me to stop wasting time and get it right. The right people were placed in my life and I went back to school to get my graduate degree in business administration. One of the young students at my children's summer camp, my daughter Chanel, became my closest asset. She kept my children while I took classes at night to complete my graduate degree. My dearest sister/friend in Palos Verdes decided to pay her housekeeper to clean my home twice a week for 6 months until things got better. This young lady was and is still remarkable! This type of kind gesture comes from deep down in the heart. It's natural, and when I mentioned this to my sister/friend a few years later, she did not remember. Thank you! Thank you! Thank you!

God is so good - He places people in your life at the right time. I am so blessed to have so many wonderful people in my life. This book will never end if I would continue to give you examples of support and God's amazing love through this challenging, yet fulfilling journey. I truly believe, when God brings people in your life for a reason or a season, they are there to fulfill the time necessary to get you back in His arms, trusting and believing in Him. My God never ceases to amaze me; he never fails us - won't you trust him.

"Because He has inclined His ear to me,
Therefore, I will call upon Him as long as I live."
(Psalms 116:2 NKJV)

Second Chances

We all make mistakes. Those mistakes deserve to be forgiven, and our God is a God of second chances. I'm so thankful that although I may have missed perfect opportunities that God had envisioned for me, He still allows me another chance. This book was supposed to be written several years ago, but I kept procrastinating. Finally, I thought I was ready - I had the book named and everything planned out. I was devastated after realizing that someone had literally written my book "Living After Losing A Loved One". I looked at the name and abruptly felt that I missed my calling. My grandmother always said, "When God gives you a vision, you better take it". If not, He will give it to someone else. This was stuck in my mind. I asked God for a second chance at getting it right. I needed another opportunity to write and touch the heart of those in need - to give me a new direction. The initial vision for my book was my memoir of every step and every feeling I encountered when I lost my husband. Well, here I am today with my story "Living After Losing" and a for sure NEW direction. I realize now, that God didn't take the vision away and it wasn't that he didn't bless me. It's just different than I thought. Yes, the plan was still there, but it was His timing, not mine.

This is my testimony. When I thought there was no way, God made a way. He brought me through a very dark journey that made me want to give up several times. I had to learn that there isn't any journey God has for us that is too big or too late. We just have to trust and believe that our God is faithful.

Our Father awaits us to come to Him and trust him. I believe He was preparing me to give Him the glory. My story, His Glory. One thing I know for sure, throughout this journey, I was the face out in front of my family with my dreams and my fears. It wasn't only about us, it was about Him, our Heavenly Father. It was about second chances and getting it right. It was about patience, trust and knowing that all things are possible for he who believes. *"I can do all things through Christ who strengthens me"* (Philippians 4:13) is the scripture that saved me. I focused on it day and night. It reminded me of how awesome our God is. All we need is to believe and trust Him. When I started feeling like it was impossible, His word reminded me that anything is possible. I started truly believing it. Yes, my God is an amazing God! He is a God of second chances. He brought me through such a very dark and long journey. I am a living testimony. Without Him, I am nothing.

"For I know the plans I have for you, declares the Lord,
plans to prosper you and not to harm you,
plans to give you a hope and a future."
(Jeremiah 29:11 NIV)

Conclusion

Denying our emotions, fears and truths usually leads to self-destructive behavior. When we acknowledge our feelings of loss and our emotional state, we can better attend to it and move forward. Understanding and accepting our state of mind is the first step to the healing process, so remind yourself that it's okay to feel sad, disappointed and hopeless.

As stated earlier, these are all natural consequences when your life path changes abruptly in a direction that we did not want. It will also help to write down your feelings, and why you are feeling this way. I remember keeping a journal, jotting down feelings and writing short letters to my deceased husband. It was very comforting, although years later, finding that journal and reading my state of mind back then, brought back lots of memories. I was able to see how truly broken I was. These memories never go away, yet the wounds have gone through a healing stage.

Although losing may be painful, frustrating and exasperating, remember that feelings of loss can become an opportunity to grow. These feelings can direct you toward what really matters to you and can be the first step in creating a more fulfilling life. Remind yourself that although you may feel your circumstances are out of control, you still can control how you react to them. Go on, **Dare to Live!**

"Blessed are they that mourn; for they shall be comforted."
(Matthew 5:4 KJV)

Epilogue

Many of us have experienced some type of loss and I know all too well, the emptiness felt inside when losing. I have had several losses and my most devastating was the loss of my beloved husband. Before taking this journey, I had spoken to so many people about losing someone very dear to them or simply something they may have been connected to and lost it. Have you ever lost someone or something that was dear to you?

I have come to realize that losing is not always about a death. Losing can be from many circumstances (i.e., loss of a family member due to their choice of life styles, a marriage that's gone sour, a relationship with a significant other, a parent, a child, a friend, a brutal death, a traumatic accident, a child that's no longer connected to the family or even from losing our jobs, homes and/or pets). A loss is a loss and many times it's absolutely the hardest thing one may endure. It's no wonder most people's first choice regarding pain tends to be avoiding it altogether. Avoiding pain and hardship in this life is less likely and therefore, learning how to deal with that pain and anguish is inevitable.

At one stage of my life, while sharing this testimony, it would literally take me back to that very day of the sudden experience in losing someone very dear to me. Our eight incredible years together before that unforgettable day, January 30, 1998, my beloved husband Edward, had an unexpected massive heart attack four days after our son was born. What was most challenging is the fact that my husband was not sick and I became a widow in a matter of less than 30 minutes. The other challenge was becoming a single parent of two small children. Jade, my daughter was age 6 and Justin, my newborn son, was just 4 days old. God knew that this was absolutely the last thing we thought would ever happen to our family, but then again, isn't that when everything seems to happen, when we least expect it?

A short time ago, I became aware rather abruptly of my primary goal as a survivor. I knew I was destined to write my story. I began experiencing feelings of loneliness and of not being enough. While allowing these feeling to overpower my thought processes, my mind and circumstances, depression and feelings of loneliness began to damage all aspects of who I was. I allowed myself to settle into a state of no control, but through the grace of God, I realized that we are biologically wired to feel lonely sometimes. Although painful, this type of loneliness was situational and subsided with time.

As time passed, I no longer focused on writing or even thinking of my loss because it would always take me back to that place of void. However, there always seem to be this very soft voice whispering, "Share your story". It seemed impossible at that time because of my struggles and trying to hang on as a single parent. A few years later, while working directly with the community and public, I began to indirectly counsel young women and men as they pursued careers, experienced loss and many other personal trials in their lives. Through these experiences, my passion for speaking and motivating individuals became my go to when I was not at my best. I began planning and coordinating walks for the American Heart Association, the March of Dimes, fundraisers and other charitable events which became my focus on and off the job. Over the past few years, together with the many teams that I had the pleasure of spearheading, we were able to raise over $250,000 in an effort to make a difference in the lives of others.

This journey has only pushed me further into serving and helping people. What better way to encourage people to *Live after Losing*?! Many people, like myself, struggle when they lose the people they love. Not only the loss of a loved one, but simply losing in all aspects of life. After all, a loss is a loss. Through many years of procrastination, I decided to start writing again. As I move forward into expectation and claim the success for my book, I believe, that *Living after Losing* will become a tool of excellence where people from all walks of life will be able to use it. I still say, "Grow through what you go through" as a way of accepting challenges. Finally, fully trust and love the life that God has blessed US with.

My prayers are that you will enjoy the ride and get what is needed to set you free while reading this book. I dare you to take control of your life. I dare you to live once again.

> *"Behold, I send an Angel before thee,*
> *to keep thee in the way,*
> *and to bring thee into the place*
> *which I have prepared"*
> (Exodus 23:20 KJV)

Acknowledgements

This book would not have been possible without some of the most amazing people who have played an integral part in my life during and after this journey. I am a great believer that it takes a village – this book is no exception:

To my Savior, King, and Provider:

Thank you, Lord! There is no one like you and I'm so very thankful to you, God, for lighting my path... I love you and thank you for the many blessings, those known and unknown. You are my forever and ever.

To my children, Jade and Justin Shepherd:

You are the delight of my life! You are a gift from heaven and a joy to parent. You love me unconditionally, support me and unequivocally, you make me unreasonably happy. Thank you for not letting me give up during this writing process. Thank you for always, always readily able to be there whenever necessary. Much Love!

To ALL the pastors who have been a part of my growth –
Thank you for all the teachings. No words will convey my
gratitude; I have learned so much from you.
Thank you, thank you, thank you!

To my Publisher:

Many thanks to Dr. De'Andrea Matthews, Founder and CEO
of Claire Aldin Publications, LLC. Thank you for the time
you have put into this amazing journey. Thank you for your
kindness and your patience. I am forever grateful.

To my friends: Deborah Yeborah, Susan Burton, Dawn &
Patrick Lombard, Aretha Matthews, Deborah Hauser and
Cynthia Jennings:

Thank you all for being such good friends, listeners and
being there when no-one else was. Your passion, sacrifice,
commitment and loyalty always blow me away. I am still
thanking God for blessing me with your presence in my life
and for you being an integral part of one of my hardest
journeys. Thank you!

To my siblings (Rebecca, Diana, Keith, Thelma and Debra):

Families are the rich soil from which we have grown and to which we return for the nourishment of our roots.
I love you ALL so very much!

To Chalon Lenard, Karen Owens, Charity Turner and Asia Lawrence:

You have been in my corner cheering me on during this writing process; Karen, you were with me during my struggle. Your prayers, encouragement, wisdom, and comical personalities were a gift. Thanks a zillion!

About the Author

After surviving her own tremendous loss, Bernice Hill-Shepherd now helps others navigate through their pain and personal trials. She is a compassionate advocate for education, public speaker and life strategist. Author Bernice Hill-Shepherd was born in New Mexico, raised in Michigan and currently resides in Southern California.

Connect with Author Bernice Hill-Shepherd

Website: www.BsCorner.net

Email: bscrner@gmail.com

 @bc0rner

 Its Bs Corner

 Shepherd Live

 4 Bs Corner